Random Thoughts

Virginia Bourgeois

iUniverse, Inc.
New York   Bloomington

Random Thoughts

iUniverse books may be ordered through booksellers or by contacting:

iUniverse
1663 Liberty Drive
Bloomington, IN 47403
www.iuniverse.com
1-800-Authors (1-800-288-4677)

ISBN: 978-1-4401-3690-0 (sc)
ISBN: 978-1-4401-3691-7 (e-book)

Printed in the United States of America

iUniverse rev. date:4/3/2009

Are You Ready?

My written words go deeper than Cupid's arrow

Not to be read by minds closed and narrow

Can't be felt by the shallow, can't be seen by the sighted

Close this book now, but you just cannot fight it

The temptation to read these Words that reveal

Forgery can't touch; more than the definition of real

Those that cannot see beyond what someone says is there

To grasp tightly to society's help over God's given prayer

Please, suffer me no further, place this "book" on the shelf

Enter back to where you worship, you slave, to serve yourself

My poetry will make you insane it will fulfill your unknown needs

Make you take account for your pure and un-pure deeds

Make you think on a level school never taught

Make you weep, and, then to scabbed knees drop

While you're down there I ask for me humbly pray

To wake up tomorrow to a brand new day

So you can finish the truth within these pages

Now you can pass this wisdom down to all the ages

Think hard now before you decide to go on

Made not for the weak, ones' minds must be strong

Take a deep breath, hold it until your lungs burst and stay torn

What you are about to experience is your mind being reborn

Welcome friend. I see you have decided to move forward. I see my writings have chosen you. What is happening in your life right now? You must be searching. My poetry was inspired by the searching. So, how does it feel knowing I don't "know" you, yet you are my inspiration? Do you want to know what this is about? Why you are still holding it although no plot is being set? Because plots are distractions. Because everything in here is page after page of climax. Are you ready? Good, then let us free each others' minds.

Dedications:

My parents; my inspiration

Mary and John; my guidance, my light

Elizabeth; my wisdom, my calm

James and Jonathan; my strength, my knowledge

Samantha; my love, my loyalty

Nieces and Nephews; my humility, my hope

Nicoya; my forgiveness

Christian; my faith, my trust

Simple Life

Criticisms of the world litter the mind from reaching its true potential

Too hard to understand

Too complicated to be solved

Too minute to open your eyes

To the blindness

Of your self

Of your words

Contradictions of the world litter the mind from truly solving

Without answers

Can there ever truly be questions?

Are you asking me?

Well don't

I have no answers

I ask no answers

The Sight of the Blind

Behold the light that brings truth before thine eyes

Behold the dark no longer transparent is your disguise

Hidden behind walls of insecurity and doubt

Hidden in a land barren and stark

Nothing resides, nothing can breath

Nothing to dam emotions torrid as the sea

Waves crashing against the land eroding away patience

Eroding away the skeletons locked away in the basement

No key to be found, no form of release

No helping the odor of the still and deceased

The air that you breathe long before was stale

The face under the lid long before was pale

In a time where weariness was too sacred to complain

Where speech was as heartbreaking as the deaf and lame

To not see was a gift bestowed only upon the high

Above the sea, Above the land, Above the sky

Mislead Are We All

I remain trapped in a world

Where the boundaries to me

Are revealed

So I watch

Always seeing always knowing

Yet I tell nothing

I expose no one

I inform no one

I hear all the sounds

I remember all the scenes

And I am disgusted

I have failed the world

For I exposed nothing

I informed no one

In my death these will be read

In your life you will not comprehend

You cannot see

For I exposed nothing

I informed no one

The world has failed me

In a concrete prison I found no security

I could not open up

To expose anything

To inform anyone

 Day and night I sat

With knowledge not of these worlds

With emotions never before seen

As deep as they ran

No one ever knew

For I exposed nothing

I informed no one

Pointless is the mortal life

Never reaching salvation

Never feeling love

For the boundaries are there

Waiting to be exposed

To inform all

That nothing can be obtained

In a world

Where lines are always drawn

Always crossed

Always exposed

Always informing

Open Your Eyes

Random Thought 1

These tears are how much I love you

I cannot speak because of how much I care

I cannot weep because my mind is blown

My heart will not beat if you're not there

Pointless

The sun streaking my face the only caress I need

The song's hypnotic pace the only food from which I feed

Wind hovering, blowing fierce, the only embrace to take me in

The flowers surrounding my senses in them my only friend

Interacting is society's trained, society's beast

Society's form of attaching yet another leash

My scissors are sharp, the blade to be reckoned with

Strong enough to slice the string, the heart, the wrist

Pointless.

Ocean

My head

My thoughts

My creation

My nightmare

Your reality

Your injustice

Your anger

Your madness

Together we stand

Never lie down

Never divided

Just swimming

In an abyss

Of insanity

Destination

Empty is a world where tenderness does not reside

Pain so deeply heartfelt no cover big enough to hide

Sadness overwhelms me knowing there is no point to hope

No point again to reach, no point to loosen the rope

Without hope there can be no life

Without success there can be no strife

Coldness sweeping through my veins until the temple freezes

Anger crashing in, like the darker side of Jesus

Rage, so deeply felt it threatens to consume

The scent of a sweet rose in the first stages of bloom

Breath it all in until the scent drugs your lungs

Fall to the top of the world at the bottom ladder rung

Swim inside its darkness where all is the color of black

Keep giving me the world keep taking your gift back

Hatred swelling up to the size of my fist

Matters of the heart falling just short of the list

Pity for my creation, my imagination, my sin

Pity for all that contain them selves within

Democracy

Save me from myself, my own hideous mistakes

Save me from the world, help me plan my escape

From the walls that encircle me; vultures patiently waiting

While I sit in question, while my mind is debating

Closed inside, no cell can compare to the loneliness felt here

Hurt inside, yet I wait for the morrow to see one catch my tear

So they just fall, soak my skin and unite with my veins

Pumps straight through my heart, my soul, my pain

Sudden Heart Attack

Music pounding in my ears like

The dance of seduction

Being played upon my heart

Loud and harsh

Striking a chord

Deep

Deeper

It glides into my veins

Surrounded by sin

My own

To cherish, to hold

Dance it off

Faster the beat plays

The Light

Blinding me 'til there

Is Nothing

Spinning faster

And faster

Louder

Faster

Until it drowns out

Everything that

Can save me

Deafened now

I can hear nothing

Random Thought 3

Here I am surrounded by my tears

Here I stay secluded with my fears

How can I move on to tell my story?

How can I possibly see Glory?

When I am drowning

Outside the sea of loneliness

When I am fighting

Temptations harder to resist

I can't talk of getting over it, I can't tell the keys to getting past

When I can't hold on to anything I turn to Faith to bring me back

To this world

Where I see only the color of pain

To this life

Where there is nothing here to gain

No one to hold My hand, no one to help me through life's trials

That make you want to quit, and yet somehow all the while

Atomic Fusion

Beauty is my curse, poetry my sin

Without I am together scrambled I am within

Visions I behold on my mind forever stain

Grounded never floating in between I remain

Between the lines of life and all its gloriousness

Its opponent being death in it righteousness

True freedom lies in one or perhaps inside the latter

Reality sets in and I ask why does true freedom matter

I find joy in being locked away

I find myself when I'm led astray

Tell me…tell me the words only engraved upon your heart

Speak to me only when your world has fallen apart

The truest freedom will be there, not judging, not seen

Coursing through your body, your minds, your dream

There I will await you with a pencil, a stool, a pad

There you will proceed as together we once had

Opening all your gates, letting your spirit free

Finally we will join as one, not a you, not a me

Come Home

Waiting on an answer to the question I never asked

Seeing all the faces before they've been unmasked

Walking on this tightrope, trying to move straight ahead

Arms of those below keep me to the land of weakened and dead

Stronger now they pull, more determined I am to stride

Outside the wind of temptation is fierce so I lock up inside

Where nothing can come in to disturb my beaten path

Where nothing is impure except the water of my bath

Now I see the problem what is hindering my process

The solution now does not evade to conquer I digest

I'm locked so far away; I have created a prison of solitude

Where the breeze never sifts my hair the silence speaks multitudes

I want to take a stroll but still find my way back amidst the trees

The only solution to my dilemma is to rise finally to my knees

Now I Lay Me Down to Sleep

Endless words flow through this pen, this mind

Endless answers informing me of what I'll find

Slam!!!

Another door closes, another day ends

Another wall built, another defense

Drop!!

One more tear, to heal the open wound

One more day of sorrow for what lies in my tomb

Smash!

Frustrated, temper too great to lash out with

Slowly diffuse myself like a cook with flour to sift

Giggle…

Insanity is what I am reduced to when the floor is my security

Doubt is what I'm filled with when attacked is my maturity

Whoosh..

There it goes, catch it; it's your last thread

The last thing to keep you from being the walking dead

Slip.

Oops, I apologize but your hands just weren't fast enough

Your heart was not too stone, your skin not too tough

Snooze

Random Thought 4

Tables turned

Bridges burned

Wants or Needs?

To have someone drink me up as if all the wells were dry

Someone to hold me so close they soak up tears I cry

My body is my temple but no one comes to worship

No one to come and claim no one has ownership

Arms that surround me no one outside can come in

Someone to look upon me see no imperfection

My beauty to them blinds they reach for my hand to guide

Confirm there is not an inch of me that I should have to hide

A time when my confidence is not torn away by rejection

Where touching and caressing is ultimate affection

Dreams aren't unattainable fantasies take shape

Where awe and elation are the feelings I make

 Words of the past made untrue by just a simple brush

Hurt, silenced, with an unspoken hush

Feed me on a level where starved I've always been

See me through eyes of a line that will never bend

If Only

When sorrow never ceases and tomorrow never dies

When wealthy complain and the injured never cry

When betrayal is the movie that sells

 When the spirit is so quiet it yells

Bounded by knowledge, trapped by strength to survive

Hounded by memories, past and present collide

Concentration breaking, too much running through this mind

Sifting through pain and confusion until nothing is left to find

No sanity, no life, no thought, no hope, no want

Like a scarecrow in a cornfield, only placed to daunt

Always having to be the better, always choosing to follow through

Always wanted to do the latter but knowing He will not approve

So stuck am I, going against trained instinct

Waiting for His breath and mine to become succinct

Then it washes over me and I know the way to be

Going through the motions, don't thank Me

Random Thought 5

The breeze sweeps over me, darting playfully in and out my hair

Feelings of searing passion overcome no touch can compare

Caressing my skin with feathery touches light but the memory has weight

The soft scents of blossoms float all around heightening my senses

Gifts only Nature can give is more costly than all other expenses

Prince of Thieves

Slicing deep enough to close the wound

Shoveling enough dirt to cover the tomb

Opening a door that leads to no place

Smiling at a man who has no face

Tears so dry, the desert is no competition

Apologies so small they're no compensation

Hand me that knife newly sharpened on the grind

Hand me the sanity to place within my mind

Hold me close now before you let me go

Talk to me in circles before you let me know

No antiseptic, no bandage, no need to cleanse

No sorry no forgiveness no need to make amends

Sleepily I walk the rest of this road

Drowsily I search for my prince among toads

Thievery and deception is my red carpet

Please, Oh God, please won't someone stop it

The blood gushing from all the stitches sewn

The weeds in my garden once again has grown

The nightmare that I don't want to wake from

Rubber band at my wrist has my fingers numb

The hole in my center being, overwhelmed by ice

Isn't that hilarious, I say, isn't that nice

Unaddressed Letter: No Names

Scent so bittersweet like flowers on a freshly covered grave

Like the dirt, it covers my eyelids, concealed in a cave

Echoing off the walls in each chamber of ice

Tumbling off my lips falling off the "dead of night"

Spearing through the shadows of forgotten gatherings

Climbing up the wall of segregations and smothering

Gulfs of tides rocking the center of the ocean

Breathtaking view weak foundation, rocky motion

Disguised with purity, cloaked in love, protection fading

Dark steel doors open to memories, try excavating

Like an un-tuned violin you sing with precision

A flower placed inside each stitched incision

Slicing, through storms of fiery red heat

No fretting through generations' eternities to seek

Restless Tears

They fall, as loud and rhythmic as the beating of the drum

Steady never stopping, never quitting, never done

They hit hard and drench the very essence of pain

Soaking the spirit, flooding the rain

Only the blind will see them, only the deaf will hear

Raging of the storm that darkens night so black it's clear

So wide is the stream that you can cross only on tiptoes

Closer and closer the beat gets as it goes

All at once it disappears visible only to the clouded mind

Again, I stumble upon chaos in the serenity I find

Give Us This Day Our Daily Bread

As I embrace my blindness, plots to me are being shown

Games not worth playing knowledge not worth being known

Power lies not in this it lies deeper than your subconscious mind

Stored, kept in a place not to be searched, not to find

Open your lids that have remained shut, locked and boarded

See perfection of world's Darkness empty and morbid

True Beauty one can find here, true life is lived out here

A world where nothing else exists except you and your fear

Centuries of fighting futile battles now come to an end

Done are years of endless salty trails that twist wind and bend

On a face with no features a smile is always seen

The sight is sharp tongue is worse hearing keen

Open to the world I finally stand, please push me down

Thank you, now again I'm home, now again I frown

Home

Thoughts more elaborate than any known language can document

Words with no syllables

Songs with no tune, poetry with no rhyme

Speak now to me

A dress code no materials combined can produce

Bare are we all

Naked to the worlds

Shelter me now

A tree stands; no leaves, no branches

It does not sway

No life inhabits it solid frame
Grow before my eyes

A bird with no wing structure
No feathers, it does not chirp
No balance
Take flight to the skies above me

A building with no frame
No roof, no walls
No foundation to build upon
This is my domain

Eternity's Question

I hear your voice calling me; I hear your soul crying for me
I look with my eyes and scream out in frustration I can't see

I grope about in this dark cold world…to find that unspoken whisper
I spin round and round like I am trapped in a mind-made twister

Your words fall loudly on my drum less ears
I feel as if I am falling like ones un-wiped tears

Like a thick cloak of coal black clouds you surround my senses
Like a soldier awarded the Purple Heart you break my defenses

I turn around to accept your fatal embrace
And as I look up into your shadowed face

I see that I would give all worldly possessions for life with you

I would decline the offer to enter the gates of heaven too

All other things would take second place

For a numbing kiss, for just a taste

What eternity would be to lie helplessly in your arms?

To fall, hopelessly, for your spellbound charms

Like an enchanting wizard I am caught up in an unbreakable spell

Will you ever release me…I am stuck wondering only time will tell

Baby

When I sit here at my desk

And I catch myself thinking about you

I am awed

My heart is being stripped of its walls like the hide of a freshly shot deer

When I look around and I see you in my own characteristics I have less fear

To face the world and mingle with the faces that once unnerved me

I don't have to calm myself down

I don't have to take a breath

No longer stepping into the crown

No longer going to face my death

You breathe the air I cannot yet stomach

Then you come back to me and I see you are alright

You take away doubt you help me deal with my fright

This sounds confused; these emotions to us are new

Just a passing thought that I had of love for you

Random Thought 6

Why, Ohhhh, Why

Do I even try?

No need to cry

Do you hear my sigh?

Sky Blue

She stands tall and proud

Amidst all that is loud

Deafening beyond anything she can see

She doesn't need help, a hand, or pity

She is strong-made of stone

She stands tall, proud and alone

Knowledge of where she is does not to her elude

Flowers from her hands, stems and all protrude

Holding them high so I cannot see atop

Never to tire Never to stop

Never to tire Never to stop

Offering to heavens and who watch from above

She needs nothing but The Unwavering Love

Importance

If I smile will you wipe my tears?

If I am strong will you conquer my fears?

If I fall will you catch my flight?

If I enlighten will you choose Light

If I give you hope will you encourage yourself

If I am poor will you also give up your wealth?

Or, will you fall and then grasp my hand

Throw me under so atop me you'll land

Then should I hate you…Curse your name

Or, love you and your kind the same

I am Love so I will choose the latter

If I die will to you it matter

Random Thought 7

Death is warming over invading all my veins

Rendering me helpless I walk around deaf and lame

Not wanting to hear the screams of the wicked and unclean

Not wanting to walk again beside the long winding stream

That twists until insanity makes my food come right back up

How else to describe this life besides damn, this sucks

Appreciation

Two Paths to travel

One completely dark

The other

Luminously lit

Of course, by "knowledge" I take the lit one

I travelled it all the way down

I ran across something that looked like a streetlamp

But I couldn't really tell

Then I saw something that looked like a big flashlight

But, well, actually I just couldn't tell

Then I was in search of the stars

I couldn't see them I think

Or maybe I could, no, forget it I can't tell

So

I walked all the way back out and took

The dark path

The Code

Blinded by my sight

Weakened by my strength

Fed with my hunger

Shortened by my length

Content with my loneliness

Gladdened with my sorrow

Living each day to the fullest

Regretting living by the 'morrow

I am stupid with the utmost intelligence

Comforted by my insecurities

I lay awake every time I sleep

Cleansed with my own impurities

Wisdom with no knowledge

Maturity with no experience

Laughing without humor

Common with no sense

Hating with all the love in me

Passionate but never searing

Failing with all my successes

Afraid but never fearing

The joys of my life

Wrong Path

Worthless choices that leave you scarred in death

Mindless decisions that make you lose your breath

I messed up

I messed up real bad

I should've gotten out

The higher the stakes rose

I should've gotten out

No one remains

To place the blame

Except myself, I lost it all

All in the name of love

I should have gotten out

Random Thought 8

I know that you've been hurt before

I know your heart has closed the door

But lady just give me a chance

Baby, it's your turn to dance

Take my hand and walk the earth with me

Across this land, the oceans, the sea

Side by side we'll travel and I'll never leave you alone

Step lightly now into my embrace, lightly, you're home

And Then Again

I've felt the ground, unflinching and hard

I've seen the deck, your card, my card

I know how it feels to drown in no depth

I know the stolen feeling, my voice and my breath

I've pleaded and I've begged for Mercy to hound my step

For sorrow to disappear, for suffocation to loosen its grip

In the end what comes to my rescue but this pen and this pad

Happiness emanating from my being; like insanity off the mad

The strongest do break, the willful get lost

The heart will open knowing the great cost

Separated from my vessel, I cannot reach the door

Cannot erase invisible tracks cannot hope for more

To ask me brings me pain that makes living a redundant scene

In a play that was written by a villain, so cold, so mean

So I close my eyes and wish that once again I will have a wish

So that once again I will feel deep enough the poison of a kiss

I feel so much I break my own heart

I wipe my own tears I end my own start

I smile while all around me is…bleak

When the words hurt too much I can't write I can't speak

Surrendering to fate, letting cards lay as they tumble

Personifying arrogance I walk around on knees humbled

While I was growing up and reality was taught

Hope was the word of the day dreams are always sought

Mentioning how broken and winded it leaves you must have slipped their minds

Must have been shared with the rest, must have excluded my kind

Hope

Spirits of fallen soldiers still impact my being

Looking in the mirror no reflection is what I'm seeing

Blood flowing down the streets like a pointless stream

I speak a language of my own no one deciphers what I mean

Stench of rotting corpses filling my nostrils breaking down my senses

No longer do I reveal myself, many walls of defenses

Pain so deep it sears through my flesh leaving visible wounds

Many lost relationships, surrounded by love-scorned tombs

Some say, "It's better to have loved and lost, then never to have loved at all"

Real Talk: You are not asking me to leap, you are asking me to fall

Then through all the gray mist consisting of all that I know, all I hate

Blessed with your presence, you're welcome here soul mate

Leave As You Came

When I opened my eyes everything was clear

Everything was whole everything had disappeared

Tangible only to a thought of what could

Secretly I am opened to only what I should

Divinely I travel through class, color, and time

Tenderly planting seeds in body, soul, and mind

Look the other way as most are wont to do

Close your eyes when you realize it is you

I came to set free, to bring confirmation

Held in my hand is the definition of hesitation

Take my other and lead me astray

To your world full of all the yesterdays

To all that you are and fear to represent

Salute the man you looked at he is president

See him when your courage will gouge out your eyes

When your pride will be the first to knock your size

When I am just a way to achieve what you can't want

What you can't feel, you can only haunt

The scent of air is littered with death of spirit

Screams of what never had the chance can you hear it

Echo in a mind where logic does not reside

Bouncing around and around nothing behind to hide

I can catch, replace and also broaden

You've slaughtered, hated and hardened

I won't pass by with no help I leave you with a smile

The only key to get you through to the next mile

When I closed my eyes everything was clear

Everything was whole everything had disappeared

Tangible only to a thought of what should

Secretly I am opened to only what I could

Random Thought 9

I know that I upset you and apologies are a joke

I can be inconsiderate; your forgiveness is my hope

I really am sorry that at times I am like a flake

I recognize selfishness and my mistake

This doesn't change what happened but I wish this will mend

You mean a lot to me and remain my one and only friend

Feast of Saints

They talk like me, they look like me

They hold like me, they feel like me

Reflections

Reflect

Back on a time brethren was not a word

Pain was a vacation in comparison to what hurt

Speak the same tongue, walk the same weary, travelled roads

Wear me upon your shoulders and you will be clothed in fine robes

Threads woven tight enough to make the surface slick

To make the surface cling and against the flesh stick

Suffocating my pores eating away like the Insufferable virus

Rotting away my tongue I reach for the bliss of silence

Where the bells ring out my arrival and Kingdoms shout my praise

The beginning of security, the end of Mortal days

Wake Up Call

When the call of the pen drowns all other sound

I must oblige, for I am duty bound

When the silence of the soul screams to awaken

I must arise, I must be taken

Found in this ink when I know no other comfort, security

Found on this pad where emotions not hidden, purity

Found in this heart daily pretending to love, ice

Found in this mind comprehension not dawning, think twice

Serenading me to write, to document what others won't say

Their tongues have vanished, and, for them I pray

I can't speak, I am choked

I am you, I am broke

Healing is a dream my wandering thoughts cannot think

Forgiveness never forsaken taking me to the brink

Taking me down a path with no bend

On and on, it has no end

Sleepy now is as I get lie down upon this earth of thistles

Peaceful dreams elude for within my pen there lays a whistle

Random Thought 10

Sitting around I got to thinking

That maybe I'm not what He intended me to be

Walking around my heart sinking

The only thing on my mind is please forgive me

I look around and see all these faces

Not a one knows what I've done

They smile and invite me places

Can they answer questions, not just one

With my feet on the ground I move on

But can you see my frown or the mask I don

Are all things forgiven or is that something sinners hold onto

Because I'm grasping with both hands and hoping it is true

The Only Freedom

Read my words but try not to understand

Take my help with never reaching for my hand

Believe in all I say while searching for no proof

Indulge in the shelter I provide never look to see a roof

Test my strength and you will never find the extent it can reach

Ask all the questions and for the answers never seek

I come with wisdom that I can never to you reveal

Let me know what when your emotions you conceal

I cannot do more than I am sent to explain

I can't see further then my eyes will let strain

Yet…yes, yet

I feel

I feel all that the soul emits, all it encompasses

I feel the triumph of the Spirit all the tribulations the Heart surpasses

The pain you call your own is shared, it hurts the world alike

Choices you make are ours for we all have that fatal spite

Never…never

Never alone are you in a life where you are surrounded, enveloped by yourself

Accepting that you have much, many understand don't underestimate your wealth

Don't; open up to Me for I am on the same level as you

Open up to your selves; know, although even then it's not through

It is the beginning, the first sign of life and the first breath

The only beginning I've come to know, it is called Death

No You Don't

No you don't know what I am saying

Unspoken

Unwritten

No you don't know the dragons I'm slaying

Past

Present

No you don't understand me

Inside

Outside

No you don't want to unhand me

Now

Ever

No you don't know what I feel for you

Deep

Within

No you don't want to hear my truth

Soul's language

Spirit's poem

No you don't know your words have scarred me

For Life

For Death

No you don't trust I can love endlessly

Shamelessly

What a shame

Random Thought 11

I sit in my corner you sit in yours across the room

Thoughts racing yet none to put down

The pen I'm holding like a King and his crown

Yet I won't put it on and I won't let my petals bloom

Because I Care

I stand by and watch you ruin your life

I can't help but to not want to be your wife

Never would I imagine that I'd be with the walking dead

Never did I dream that the decaying would fill my head

But you do and I have no choice but to watch and wait

For that thing to take over, that thing we call Fate

It will be our undoing, it will make me go

Seen it before, not again, No!

Don't change if it is you

Don't promise if it's not true

Tell me maybe one day we can cross again

Depart not as my foe, but as my friend

Someone is Listening

Where does one reach when they cannot see?

With no voice of their own how can they plea

When lost is a comfort and loneliness a breeze

Of fresh air that, just for a moment, frees

To a place that soothes and chases demons away

Tucked inside my heart, where forever will stay

Escape from the walls that are built within

Escape from my pain, my desire, my sin

To let bitterness prevail, to let hate win

Is turning back and building up that wall again

Who would knock down Berlin just to put it back up?

Who picks up the pieces just to let them again drop?

Decisions will be made, some will come easy, some hard

You are feeling your hand is not big enough for yet another card

I know some One with a hand to lend you just have to reach out

He already heard the whisper and She can handle the shout

Needs

I don't need to hold you

I know you are there

I don't need to see you

I feel you nearby

I don't need to listen

I already heard you

Words whispered

Caressing my soul

Worshipping my entirety

I don't need to read between the lines

I already understand

Your past is mine

I've lived it every time

I look

Into your eyes; into your soul

Though tracks have been wiped away

I can feel the sting

Of the trail your tears left

Upon the face I carved

I dreamed

I kissed

I don't need to hurt you

I know my emotions have already hit you

Deep

Searing you, branding you

Like the Scarlett Letter

I wear you upon my breast

I comfort you without a touch

I don't have to know you

I already love you

Random Thought 12

Secrets to your soul shadow your eyes

So proud to wear your transparent disguise

Hidden from all, yet the blind can see

With my sight impaired blatant is your mortality

Eating away at the essence of your breath

Decaying day by day; a corpse after death

Mindless Thoughts

Wearing a mask to disguise what I feel, where I stand

Taking deep breathes yet heart and lungs never expand

Smelling the sour scent of incense floating through the air

Hear droll sounds of the organ wondering if I've been spared

Numbness overcoming me, I am still like the homeless in ten below weather

Falling apart from disappointment and pain, all the while holding it together

Repercussions happening slowly working its way idly through my bones

I cannot speak, I cannot cry, I can only sit and write these poems

The effects will wear off and one day again I will try

To climb back upon that horse whose seat is so high

To fall, perhaps, or maybe to stand tall and ride fast

Perhaps once more I will find a saddle that could last

Through all the trials and all obstacles so I can storm off into the wind

But I doubt it, I'll probably get on, run into the flames, and get singed

Hear my cry of anguish my laugh of freedom; hear the rustling of my restless soul

See me succeed, see me go all the way to the top, yet never reach my goal

Talk to me of things of the past and perhaps that will relieve the presence

Give away all belongings and come join me in the world of peasants

Don't tell me of the future for it is something I am not likely to see

With all the wrongs in the world I will be blinded by my own mortality

To Wish, for things that cannot happen, to Hope, for all that won't exist

Is synonymous with the efforts of holding water in a tightly closed fist

So, again I will sit and ponder and accept things as destiny, as fate

I will learn that I can't be arrested so I've not a need to learn escape

Situations will arise, loyalties will fall or they will bond tight

But, mental note to self: Don't ever stop the fight

How Ironic

Working hard to get ahead for the same that hold you down

Smiling in the faces of all that try to make you frown

Not knowing which way is up in an upside down society

Not knowing what your name is without your digit identity

Faceless are we all when the game of life is dissected

Shameless is the world with all the minds infected

Yesterday is just a memory that people repeatedly play

So how is it that one can claim they are living for today

Fate is for the lost, purity for the sinner

Hope for the unsuccessful endings for the beginner

Time prolongs impatience with a deadly pace

Time gives us time to regret so when does it erase

Tomorrow is a dream, yet is attained by us all

Procrastinating and incompetent always fearing the fall

Surpassing the knowledge before, stupidity never left behind

Helping only a select few, but the heart is said to be kind

Agreeing with the wisdom read and you claim you didn't know

Examples given through experience yet to you no one showed

Interesting.

As I Wonder

As I wonder and look upon all these faces

The memories once so sacred time erases

It plays a fatal game, in the vicinity of my heart

A game though against my better judgment I played a part

Now, left alone, Misery hounds my every step

At arm's length is where all things should've been kept

No direction my thoughts take as I sit here and wonder

No conclusions my heart makes while I just ponder

As I wonder and blindly chase my dreams

Further away they get each day it seems

Faith pulls me through and for nothing shall I ask

As I wonder if this is true I reach down for my mask

The Definition of "Us"

Ancient ancestors speak to me with a language of our own

Ancient graves seen by me through thick forests they've grown

Cryptic words are found yet they never get mumbled through these lips

Elusive bodies whisper secrets invisible hands never loosen their grips

Codes that go un-deciphered even though their messages are the key

Silences go unbroken language is the only bridge between you and me

Sitting in a corner pondering thoughts too deep to uncover

Searching for answers as a child searches for love from a mother

Help me unlock your closet, help me decode the tales

Without working together neither of us has prevailed

Random Thought 13

The rattling of bags

The incessant chatter of the tongue-less

The sweet scent of hysteria

Dying a Better Death

Tears running down my face, streaking my soul

Deception as deep as the river and as dark as coal

Dances around my heart to a melody enchantingly dark

Stripping me of everything, leaving me bare and stark

I cry out into the darkness, someone please hear me

Where is my company? My name is Misery.

I see crowds in the distance their ears torn from their head

No one to listen or respond to what has been said

Naked to the world is as I stand now

Loneliness running over; a farmer's plow

Normally I can dodge and evade the spinning blade

Normally, I bounce back stronger, more staid

But I cannot move, cannot budge an inch

My faithful executioner has tightened the cinch

Placed around my neck, it steals my very breath

I fear not losing my life for I already live in death

Here Are the Keys

You wiped your tears on my soul now I am forever wet

You engraved your name in my spirit I shan't forget

As they fell so did the walls that I placed around my heart

As I held you I knew you were my world not just a part

They surfaced from a well buried deep inside

Where my eyes could not see they went to hide

They shake my memory

Like an awful dream

They knock me over

Like a fierce-flowing stream

Never leave my side

I fear I will fall

Never feel alone

I'll beckon to your call

It took you breaking down for me to realize

Emotions beneath the surface in your eyes

You have the keys to my essence, my heart, my door

My dragon your breath is a fire blazing forever, no…more

I do not make promises I cannot die to keep

No wasteful tears are shed see why I truly weep

These are my vows to you I speak them with all I'm of

Here I am…with my Heart…it is Love

Eternally, I promise

Blindness

Speaketh not into my deafened ears for thy words will be hollow

Hunger is my strength for mortal food I can't tolerate to swallow

Whisper unto my soul the meaning behind your words speak now or forever hold your peace

Feedeth me only thine's richest intentions and I shall have the heartiest of feasts

Dine with me at my table that has been lavishly prepared to quench the beast

The famine of evilness, of replacing what was lost, what has now ceased

On an empty stomach I shall travel, within a weary body I remain

Pleasure a self-made mirage as long as I inhabit this domain

Take from me this breath and breathe unto another along the path

Heed my words; fight temptation or feel the inferno heat of the wrath

Not needed are keen ears to hear words spake in worldly tongues nor tender morsels you believeth you devour

Oughtn't dwell upon what is not, will never come to pass not then, not now, not even in your calendar hour

Hearing is used for alertness to all approaches, all around me

Eyesight help me rejoice in the worth of what my eyes doth see

Future will come in due time mean whilst I stop and pay respect

Not waiting, expecting, sizing…all that is not yet

Someday in the future I may look back and not remember what was seen

Constantly submerged was I in Worry, listening for any and every thing

Unforgettable scenes will be lost, chances nonexistent lacking sufficient time to change it somehow

Stop wishing on the dream about all that cannot Appreciation of life is all, necessary for the now

Whispers of Love

My Destiny,

Where do I begin? I know not what to say. I only know that thinking of you comes as often as *ma Coeur* will beat. Feeling you is a craving I have like none other. Never will my hunger of this be completely fed. *J'ai faim ma petite tete de chou.* I write now of what I feel. Deep within. Where no mortal's sinful hands can touch. Where dirt can never litter. Where pollution of no kind can exist. *Je ne l'aime pas.* For it is as pure as sunlight. Beaming upon only one although others get the rays. Touching upon their skin as a mother touches a babe. The caresses I leave upon you I do with utmost care. As to not disturb the serene beauty I have found. *Je vois le soleil dans vos yeux.* I grasp it. Never wishing to let go. Holding on forever yet learning to give you space. *Je ne veux pas a.* Your kisses give me comfort. Your voice is a sweet melody. Only my soul knows the song. *Chantez pour moi.* To you I shamelessly give my control. *Vous etes ma vie.* I give to you the breath of life. The breath of a white dove soaring on the wings of the breeze. The hands of the earth. In all its wisdom. Carry it along to the freedom of the spirit's domicile. *Allons-y.* There we stay. Contented for all eternity.

Je t'aime.

Random Thought 14

Sing to me because I need to hear your voice

Come to me I need to know I have the choice

Because I'm trapped in a world where I just can't see

Because I'm lost in the reality of what can't be

I can hold in my hands but they feel real

Walk With Me

Two paths crossing two hearts searching

Two minds knowing two souls hurting

No connection can be seen when the eyes are too wide

No direction found when following maps of the outside

The travel is long but never weary

The road is dark but never dreary

There is no light from this tunnel to shine

Wisdom, innocence, purity is what you find

Part now and tread, onto your personal path

The isolation of loneliness in time that will pass

Destiny awaits the seekers who need not look

No light, just a throne, and a book

The Scent of a Woman

Always comfortable but never at ease

Always confident always on your knees

Always knowing, never relaying

Always living while slowly decaying

Always giving, have nothing to spare

Always despising can't help but to care

Beaten spirit, strengthened soul

Embrace to light the way, Heart to fire the coal

Confused mind, knowledge surpassing generations

Always doing wrong possessing one not many temptations

The scent of a woman

The Garden

Located in my garden beside the rotting corn

Lays my pen and pad, attached its fierce horn

When it blows the tomato leaves wither and fall

The seeds dry and no juice it makes none at all

The carrots bright orange glorifies the puddle of red

That surrounds the stems digging up the silence of dead

Potatoes beneath the surface many eyes to watch below

Only one to escape the freezing of the bitter winter snow

My Forever?

Do I say I love you enough, do I help you dream?

Do I make you laugh enough or is your memories my scream?

Do I lift your spirits to unreachable depths and heights?

Make your hope flourish and your soul take flight?

Do I offer enough consoling, do I understand your mind?

I can only hope for a yes to each, all I can say is I try.

Give Me a Moment

Why am I wrong to want to be loved my way?

Why do I have to silence my needs?

Why is love what is convenient for you?

I stay home because I have you again.

I stay awake because I can see you again.

I trust in you to see me and what I need.

I trust in you to deliver as you promised.

Only as you promised.

Nothing more.

Never more.

I just want to talk.

I just want to hold.

I just want to smile.

I just want this to work.

Why is that wrong?

The Day of the Dead

Whisper sweet nothings to a face with no ears

See pain from these eyes unable to shed tears

Shield me from the world rotating on a crooked axis

Spin me around, charge for the ride, add on taxes

Hold me with arms that don't stretch too wide

Give me a window to view but lock me up inside

Where Darkness is my friend and my companion is named Lonely

Here is where I am meant, just me, one, no, only

Embracing all my ignorance with the thirst of hungry wolves

Sit me upon your horse let me fall trample me with the hooves

In a skin tight heat the blaze selflessly melts away the flesh

Melts away thoughts, the heart beating inside the chest

In my mind Insanity comforts me like an old foe

Like a book with blank pages a story never told

Comprehension never dawning, never obtained, never to reach

Never to tire, never to stop, never to receive anything but grief

Judge Not Yourself

Through life we travel many roads

Surpass many tribulations

Through pain we learn many joys

Through error we learn to fight temptations

Judge not yourself

Through God we find our rightful path

Through tears we see who we truly are

Through smiles we cry for the entire world

In solitude we travel far

Judge not yourself

Through decisions we find the difference
Between what we want and what we need
Through failures we obtain what it takes
To repeat history or to succeed

Judge not yourself

Through friends and family we find support
Stronger than any steel bridge that can be built
Through love for us we find forgiveness for others
Through humbleness on our knees together we knelt

Judge not yourself

Through good intentions we are blessed
Through bad intentions we are taught
With God watching over us every battle can be won
Even defining ones that are inwardly fought
Judge Not Yourself

Solutions

Words spoken from a brain-dead mind
Never lost a thing but still looking to find
Open up one's soul to find a cryptic being
Having all answers never comprehend the meaning

Save thyself from harm yet throw your heart into the fire
Throweth thy poisonous darts, rest but never retire
Hardships of the living, secrets owned by the dead
Lie down on the floor escape the innocent-looking bed

In a crowd I am surrounded by a loud isolation

My actions not my words are society's creation

Molding me into something that has no title, no name, no face

Sending me on a journey to no home, no stableness, no place

Through all this I find a light that is as small as a spark

Through the murky silence I hear a lullaby in the dark

Singing a sweet soft melody spinning me around in a pleasant dance

Asking me to leap off, but I find myself, scared to take the chance

In a standstill we wait for the doors to be opened, for the gate keeper

We walk forth and I am drawn back in to the embrace of the grim reaper

I feel his poisonous grasp all along my spine, my body is getting stiff

Unknowingly to him I creep over towards the edge of my dominant cliff

Closer and closer I crawl, louder and louder my song plays again

Now I am faced with a dilemma as I scrape nearer to the end

Stay with what I know; all that my memories let me recall

Or take one more step and feel the mind numbing heat of the fall

My palms are sweating acid and my mind is raging with illusions

Indecisiveness is not my flaw, but for once I find no conclusions

The beating of my heart falls loudly upon my ears THUMP THUMP THUMP THUMP

I turn around into the embrace of darkness; I stop, step back, and jump

Of Course

The rose you gave me last night pricked my finger

The necklace you brought me left a rash

The picture you took with me got caught in the fire
Now I am stuck only looking at ash

The mirror you got me broke
Reflection only comes through in sections
An eye here, a tear there, a smile in one
Then a frown, yes this is my reflection

The DVD player ate our favorite movie
The CD we loved is scratched and cracked
The dinner we made together is burnt
The purse you purchased me got snatched

But we still love, don't we?
As strong and as fierce as we met?
I am still like your rain, am I not?
When ablaze I'm still there to keep you wet?

Of course I am, you always tell me so
I am overreacting I am blinding myself
I am imagining all this poverty
While I am basking in all this wealth

And nothing has changed right?
Everything is as it was in the start
We have the keys to each other's soul
We know the doors to each other's heart

Yet, I feel no draft

Random Thought 15 (Utopian Passions)

You close your eyes and open your heart
Feel my tongue across your lips, you part
Breaths mingle; you feel the rising of my heat

Relax, let go, lie down as if to sleep

Gazing at your nudity…mmm…I hunger to taste your flesh

From your mouth down your neck and lavish your chest

Circling your nipple like a lion circles its prey

Opening my mouth incoherent words I say

I delve lower nibbling at the crevices of your frame

As I take you in my mouth I hear…shhh…no names

Swirling around your member like an unending whirlpool

Rubbing tenderly on life noticing for me that they are full

Lower yet still I travel meandering leaving trails like acidic rain

Repeating all I go back up my body upon yours does stain

Once again I encounter the soft glow in your eyes

While we lay entranced breast to breast thigh to thigh

Flip me over onto my back and raise above me…like…my King

Shudder with knowledge of skill, how you make my body sing

Placing your fingertips on my eyelids commanding them to close

Placing tender kisses upon my lips, my ears, my nose

You slaughter my senses with your mind-numbing strokes of practice

I scream…for more, just a tease will never for me suffice

Your hands travel down in a flaming path to my…

Trained

My mind brings haunting pictures to taunt my worthless soul

My fears are no longer for they are all your achieved goals

To change my thoughts are pointless to go with them drives me insane

When I broke down all my walls you proceeded with your lock and chains

Turn around, don't look, push me so I don't fall

Leave me my barren world don't answer when I call

I speak with conditioned tones none go straight to the soul

I asked you for forever now I have found what's to be my toll

Alone I was with fears nightmares couldn't compare to

You are beside me now however temporarily it is true

I see films behind my eyes that never can be revealed

Doubt, questions, a frightening reality is my playing field

They run over in my mind, I add confusion to thicken the plot

I hold on unforgiving to my forever never wanting it to stop

What I lose in return is grand to apply a preferred label is the key

Won't document its title for I no longer want you to have all of me

Suppressing those awful episodes I will once again return to the stage of life

I will be strong, successful, supportive, the irony of the perfect wife

Feel Me

To be served a platter by a gimp hand, I am King

To be connected so purely, please cut my string

I listen to your song because you don't feel the words deep

I do not sing to you, the vocabulary here is not steep

You tell me you love me because your heart is hesitant

I tell you that I am leaving, to you better time spent

You search endlessly for me; to see my beauty in disguise

I crave loneliness to see your magnificence with closed eyes

You tell me to take note, best for me it is said to be

I try not to teach, know, deaf hear, blind see

You take my words unkindly; Pain is the gift I bring

I speak harshly to the core present classification: Unforgetting

Smile you say waiting for muscles to join and lift

I weep instead healing I thought to be the best gift

Now where?

Sunset

As it towers over me, never do I lie here in the dark

Hovering, clothing my every piece, nude not stark

Light showering my members, flourished they become

Separate entities for a moment in time become one

In its brightest hour it scorches deep into my core

Never cinching always leaving room to want more

Then it begins to dull, fading like memories of the travelled roads

Unsure why, like an analyst deciphering the most cryptic codes

Slowly it gets stolen by the night sky across and above

As temporary, as permanent, sunsets, love

Horizons

Just like the waves I release from this pen

Dark is suffocating this domain, this den

Crashing into it every turn, every chance

Slashing right through I'm of stone it of glass

Though the reverse the un-blind see at a glance

Amuses it does, eventually the emotions will pass

Just like the Story, it will end

The One that Mercy will send

Trudging up the sand until the bottom to me is clear

This ink pulling at all of my hopes igniting all the fear

The calm is here for it does not appear

The dawn is lighting my way back here

Back to the beginning

Random Thought 16 (Searching)

Time and again I have found myself just sitting off by the side trying to make sense of my life. Why am I here? Why can't I go? I search endlessly for answers I already have. Knowing the answers and knowing how to apply the answers is where I keep falling short. With all the trials and tests I go through on a daily basis, it is hard for me to understand when to apply what I know. So, in the end, I sit off by myself once again lost within my own self. Searching, always searching. We search for Love, for Purpose. We search for Acceptance from others, from ourselves. We spend our whole lives searching for all of these things, yet we always smile, always laugh. We search for Truth, for the Right Path to walk, yet we know the feeling of Guilt. I cannot help you with any answers to these searches. I can only provide you Companionship.

Distract Me Quick

You put me upon a pedestal built with arthritic limbs

You sang to me of tunes banished from the hymns

Banished from the light, exiled from the sweet

Dancing upon my head thinking from soul to feat

Triumph for the lonely galloping away from the sea

Away from all the wisdom that is often told by me

Swim along my banks, peek at the coral beneath

Tread towards the edge, towards the drop, the deep

Glistening under the surface a shell awaits the snare

The capture of the conqueror the ending to the dare

Paddle back to the beginning and let the foolishly sighted awe at your find

Couldn't you handle the deep? Whispered to the creases of your mind.

Sunshine

Lighting up my world so subtly I am washed away in your rays

In complete euphoria is how I spend all of my present days

Times have gotten rough and smiles seemed hard to reach

The walls around my heart you soon did accomplish to breach

Eyes as green as the trees which bring life to this earth

Heart as pure and delicate as a child just conceived at birth

Perhaps my words don't tell the depth of emotions my eyes convey

Perhaps I will learn to better show you one of these days

That I am not wrapped around your finger but my soul is wrapped around your hand

Thanks you for giving me the opportunity of being your one and only man

Drink It All

Once again going crazy, once again going numb

Once again weeping once again I'm coming undone

Faster it spins its web to sink and drink my blood

Faster it strikes me dead until I become a smudge

Where is my rope, my thread to sanity, peace of mind?

Where now is the out to this maze, which way will I find

Walls eat away at my flesh these memories torment my psych

These journeys that I travel, I cannot take only the dusty hike

Time ticks by and waits circling till you come back around

Life attached to hands of the ones with the leash, the hound

Break those chains and run, trip upon the dead that did not make

Run through this forest of tombs to the ones who will not wake

The sun shines on the horizon, now I am forever blind

The ray that looks so innocent is like poison for the mind

Just Breath

Can you taste the freedom; it is destined to approach?

Can you taste the right to speak on idle thoughts never broached?

Like poison, it runs down your throat burning, like whiskey

Your body rejects it, your soul searches for it endlessly

Blindly groping through mazes, blocked at every corner

Surrounded by familiar faces but always being a foreigner

Pasts too different to coincide, to unite

Will too lost to stand up to the repetitious fight

But with the 'morrow comes the scent my body craves to caress

Hunger for the pain, the remorse, the distress

Then the clouds part and the ethereal light beams

Meandering over my flesh like muddy watered streams

With depths that can hide bodies too lost to be found

Too deep to see the cries too far below to hear the sound

Too scared to swim beneath to find what was never really there

Never really intimidating, never really worth the scare

Smells Good.

Vana

Sweet girl hide not from roaming eyes

Fear not judgment, ridicule or despise

Move your body to touch my soul

Touch my heart for it can't be sold

A name I needed to go with the innocent face

The searching eyes to me seemed out of place

Out of this world you constantly try to reach

Hardened hearts, walls one cannot breach

Smile once again, but this time not for me

For yourself once you've gained sight to see

The words I speak are incomprehensible to you now

Open Heart and Mind, and I will show you how

To reach heights unknown to your unnourished mind

Look deep within and understanding of this you will find

I Cannot

Fear courses through my veins igniting blood

Loneliness engulfs me like a fast current flood

Tears streaking down my soul leaving nothing dry

Hear my pleas for Content, someone hear my cry

Sweet bird outside my window

Sing to me of forgotten tunes

Large tree save room at root for me

For my not yet dug tomb

I think with blank thoughts

I write with empty words

This pen I once again hold

Salve put upon my burns

Deeper they eat into my tortured flesh

Like a virus consuming all

Soon I'll hear the cracking of bones

Again I have taken the fall

Court's Jester

Once again we travel back to see my flesh in the guillotine

Ready to drop, ready to slice, swift, and clean

What crime have I committed but being true to self?

How many times I've repented all my misspent wealth

I hear my final words being read to a transparent crowd

I hear shouts for Death, chanting in my mind getting loud

I cannot speak; around my mouth is their weathered bind

Cannot convey my message it will die trapped in this mind

Trapped in this heart, pumping through clogged veins

Quietly the blade drops my vessel now without name

I pause before my exit before I continue onto my second chapter

To look below at those looking upon my sin with laughter

How funny is ignorance I ask, how funny is changed fate

How hilarious does this strike that you all heard too late

Pick Me

Silent expectations of the boastfully loud

Humbly dip my head to those that seek Proud

Always bend my will when it seems to others I am a fool

Offer me leather couches place beneath my wooden stool

Comforts and luxuries, individual perceptions, definitions

Thoughts of past and future, present is just reminiscent

Talk of old, sight of new, heart of hope and light

King of all, King of none, together in this fight

Side by side, defending all that exists, all truth divine

All hate and discomfort slaughtered, freedom truly mine

Opening up wounds just to be sure blood still flows

Opening up minds just to be sure that it stays cold

Chilled and served like most dishes served at prestige

Harboring thoughts and emotions some die and not seize

Never hold to their bosom, nourish, plant and grow

I'll be willingly at the bottom, always the last to know

Random Thought 17 (Loneliness)

Some poems I write at times where only the pen and paper existed. The only comfort I was to find in an uncomfortable world. When Solitude was an enemy that I could not shake. Peace was the thing that wreaked the most havoc on all of my senses. I craved love, attention and whatever else someone could give me that would make me feel "special". Most times I know that I am already special. But, then loneliness sweeps in and erases all that I know. This is why I prefer the pen. No erasers. No mistakes. What I crave is a temporary solution to a problem that will always exist. I need a friend is what I tell myself. I need a companion is what I swear I feel, I know. Then, on my search for the true way of life I encounter Loneliness and every time I am its willing victim. Every time I am left numb with the knowledge that this was not it. This was not the answer. But, then I know no other answer. So, I write. With my pen.

Traumatized

Pain rising off your body penetrating to my core

I wish I could heal your heart I wish I could do more

What world do I live in that would wound a soul so pure

What strength I see in a man that has survived, endured

What tests you have been put through your perseverance I admire

Fiery deception that leaves you robbed, raped, and tired

I feel it all as if to me the crime was committed

As if I was the victim, as if I had submitted

Accepted all the wrong to the point I can no longer hope for right

What is Faith worth when you're losing the will to go on and fight?

This tear I shed for you to salve the pain

This sob I suppress, this Anger I tame

Never knowing why, your control never failing never slipping

Sanity through this grip, elusive, always barely gripping

Alienation

How do I begin to describe indescribable pain?

Deeper than blood, than the path of the vein

Support so superficial always easy to replace

See this shining smile pasted to a perfected face

See what I project then doubt I can wear a disguise

The smile and face would fade if you noticed these eyes

You swim inside them and those that cannot, drown

You don't see scars because too well I don the crown

I placed atop my head to help hold the façade in place

The innocence below I hid; He will never let you take

Try as you may, failure will be your only success

Breezy as the wind your effort to me didn't stress

Crucified for the Morals taught to me direct

For them I sacrificed, let them slice my neck

Deep enough that Wisdom and Truth are my breath

Love makes relevance, their price, only Death

I begged to pay; I prayed my currency was sufficient

My next man uncomprehending only noticed the distance

Where they chose not to go because their soul is not too strong

In this life they are revered because here is the places they belong

From birth I was separated, from life I intertwined

What was in my heart with the unfortunate in my mind

See what you can't visualize every time upon me you gaze

Don't extend your hand I've walked, lived and loved this blaze

Let it singe, let it spark, let it go through all three layers

Only then will you catch a glimpse of the contents of my prayers

Love's Name

When I watch you leave I pray that you're not gone long

When you're here it seems as though I only see the wrong

I wish I knew how to take things back to when I couldn't get enough

When our relationship was easy to keep when life made things tough

I hate how I make you feel, when I see self disgust on your face

To know I rarely speak of love, hate and regret taking place

Makes me hurt and feel life giving up on what I know we could be

For some reason I feel trapped, pleaded and begged to be free

Then you go away for a moment in time, Separation like Death

You unlock the door and it feels like someone handed to me Breath

I remain confused and lost, which direction am I to turn

I try what I know and it seems I still feel a bit of the burn

Then we love and you fill me with all of your soul

I think, "Why would I ever let go?"

I speak with venom lacing my words, pain painting your face

I pray I try to get better at not making you feel second place

Then I fail and put us back on shaky ground

I can't figure how to see the man I once found

I know we are falling apart and I keep saying that you're the blame

I am wrong too, but I do not know how to express my self-shame

Love me in a way I don't know, exist in a man

I find criticism and gently slap away your hand

Can't speak these words, they come close to my heart

Baby, I apologize for not always playing my part

Shamelessly I beg don't ever leave, of course I want to be Wife

Waking in final hour looking over noticing you're still my Life

Please, help me be what you need.

Been There, Done That

Lock me in the closet, punish me until I repent

Trample my face in the dirt until all faith is spent

Offer me your hand and ask me why for it I do not reach

Speak beyond time wonder why I shun greatness we teach

Hold me to your bosom until all breath is lost

High sum for comfort when life is the pricey cost

Ask me why I love, and accept only my scorn

Read to me from the book where every page is torn

Ripped from the very seam, separated from the rest

Stories told on those pages are sure to be the best

Tell me a joke with no punch line so my laugh can lack heart

Speak of forever togetherness making sure actions tear apart

Ask me why Hope no longer light these empty eyes of mine

Ask me, why I refuse to share now the me that is truly divine

Covered with the cloak only worn by the dismal and grim

See what my world consists of when my walk of choice is sin

Down me for my rights, hate me for my knowledge they exist

Reject my tender affection then turn to me for my kiss

From lips that now only speak wicked because holy was unappreciated

To the lost, the trapped, the yesterday me this is written and dedicated

Company

I'm haunted by these tears that drown all there is

All there can ever be, all sadness, all bliss

Lies and deception served with my eggs and toast

Slow burn starting from inside, singe, roast

Laugh at me King, Laugh at me Duke

I entertain under these lights until I puke

Stages, scenery and characters change but the hot light stays

Regardless of the time of the nights, the time of the days

The bewitching hour you hear of is here, it is the now hour

Why else would the aftertaste of life always seem so sour?

Bitter, on a tongue that doesn't exist, not even a muscle, a speck

Hatred swirling like the chain for my tongue worn about your neck

Like chains forged in steel, hard to break apart

Hard to scar the soul, hard to break the heart

Steel and Stone make the world I inhabit cold to the bone

I'd welcome you in, offer a seat, alas, there is no home

Enigma

Haunted memories, buried skeletons, all things you try to hide

I never hear you slay them; I do behold them in your eyes

You search for something in you, you feel you cannot find

You recognize you're ahead you let guilt of Failure hold behind

You open up like a flower that knows it is soon going to wither and die

You're an eagle grounded for you don't have faith in your ability to fly

So grown, through life's' trials you've guarded yourself tighter than a jail

You are strong, you are wise, you are uncommon yet you still are frail

You control all that can be and then try all that cannot

You've fires that burn within yet fear when it gets hot

I don't have knowledge of you, but I do, for I feel the same history

You're my brother, my child, though others see you as a mystery

Secret Society

I travelled to a world where everything was right

Everything was one, no struggles, no fight

In its purest form I found beauty undisturbed, untouched by man

Stronger than anything we know there it lies, no, it stands

Majestic, proud, with the knowledge of all it is

Sun spotlights it where the rain upon it will kiss

Breathing in will cleanse the soul, cleanse the body, the mind

No need to search for perfection, for there that is all you'll find

Life is all around, vital, breathing and secure

Poison in our walls in this haven you'll find the cure

Smaller than you've ever felt this place will make you know

You are minute, you are trespassers, although

In their green outstretched arms they welcome all who dare

To open up and be free to show you that you really care

We are taught to close up but there we will learn to open

Hold our tongues but voices here are strong, outspoken

Then they come upon your senses in a melody soft and sweet

So I come upon these grounds where you and I will meet

The only of our kind so the only who understands this place

The One who sees how gorgeous things are that have no face

It calls to my innermost beings it begs it to come within

It shows me where I can go to find worlds without sin

A world that never betrays, cheats, or inflicts pain

This world may get torn down but in heart remain

Comfort Zone

You reach to grasp my hand with a decrepit finger

You smile and I can't help but to see what lingers

The scowl, the frown, the disappointment in your eyes

Your soul, your true emotions that you cannot help hide

Like a mirror, I stare at you, our reflection

Like an outcast I'm shunned from Tenderness and Affection

Daddy, I know everything you do has a rhyme, a reason

Every time it rains, snows every change of every season

Never doubt it's meant to happen never care to ask why

I cannot hold on forever, yet I can never cry

Pain inside never surfaces never to this world itself reveals

All the superfluous times I try never helps, never prevails

Reach deep into my soul and there they answer lie

Now I sit and reflect, then receive a heavy sigh

I know my place, in hell's furious blaze

Control from running into the mortal-fulfilling craze

Suppressed are my feelings even though the sun upon me now shines

Exhaustion overcomes me, but for now I would like to take the time

Listen its Father, His Wisdom, guide me

Never to be seen, protect me, hide me

Take me home to the land where I know I'm never exiled

Hold me now, I need you, I am your child

I come with humble wishes I know that you'll grant

You keep me strong when my own Spirit can't

When I stumble upon the small and never notice the large

When I feel the ripping of battle and never remember the charge

I fall back upon the only net I am provided on this earth

The knowledge of my heritages, my nations, my birth

To you I dedicate my lives as I know you do yours

You come upon this hospital and bandage all sores

That exists within this vessel which was given with care

So thankful to begotten daughter to always feel you there

Now I shall enter back into this purpose with the un-showing stare

I will seek you again, and for now, I will end this sinner's prayer

Perseverance

What is God?

God is Love.

What is Love?

Completeness

When all the voids and emptiness have been filled

Filled with everything you are

And everything you can never be

What is Laughter?

It is the rainbow after the downpour

It is the soul letting you know

Everything will be OK

What am I?

I am you.

We are one.

Though I have never seen your face

Never felt your touch

Never comforted you

I have

Can you feel me?

Can you feel yourself?

What is fear?

It is the darkness

Pulling you away from the light of God

What is jealousy and envy?

It is you questioning who you are

What are you worth?

In turn

Questioning who I am

And what I am worth

Signifying

Who is God?

And what is his entity worth

What are questions?

They are you

Blinding yourself to the answers

That you already have

Already know

And feel within

What are you?

My brother, my sister, my child, my guidance

You are my every thing

What is faith?

The only weapon you need

Against the questions

The jealousy

The envy

The darkness

The only thing that protects you

In an unprotected world

It is the only road to travel

To achieve

Perseverance

This is dedicated to those who have never found god. Or have and cannot fully accept him. To everyone I know and everyone I do not know, for in reality I know you all. Your sins are mine. And I have already prayed for forgiveness. He hears you. Love god's servants' vsb.

Wrong Turn

They fall

And the salt upon my lips

Now burn

I am weeping

For my sins

I am weeping for the world

In darkness I walk

I now fear the light

That once brought me salvation

Now causes me to be shamed

I have no more fears

For I am numb

I cannot feel fear

For I cannot feel

Father forgives us our sins

For we know not what we do

Random Thought 18 (Exhaustion)

Imagine working a nine hour shift on three hours of sleep. When you return home you cannot catch up on rest because you've got a little one waiting on you to nurture. Tired. Not to be confused with exhausted. Exhausted is when you don't even have the energy to hope for a better tomorrow. When you cannot ask for rest. Tired affects your body. Exhaustion affects your mind and soul. You don't want the answers to the questions you've asked yourself all your life. Trying to live up to all the silent expectations. The kind of expectations that are screamed so softly you swear they will walk away with your sanity. Everyone expects something out of you. Exhaustion is attained when you try to achieve other's expectations. So, then what? What to do about the expectations. Ignore them? Find a better way to achieve them? No. It is none of these. Know that all that is expected of you, you have already attained. You have achieved something more than anyone has ever expected. That is how true exhaustion comes about.

Apology Not Accepted

A ring made of gold I cannot give

A heart with its likeness I can

Promises that can be broken I won't give

Good intentions held in this hand

Yet I cannot guarantee I won't fail

With my last breath I will fight the fall

I cannot fight all your battles and win

Now I will stand with you through it all

I cannot give you the world or riches beyond the skies
I can give you all in my world comfort all of your cries

I can feel the depth of your pain
Replace broken memories with ones to last
I can't say you will never again hurt
I can only try and help you learn to really laugh

I can't erase the wrongs that I've done
I'm sorrys to me just don't work
I can only be joyous when you're happy
Feel ashamed when I cause hurt

Forgive me now for all that I might do
When my tears fall and streak my face
The taste of salt upon these lips of mine
Within your heart I still have a place

My Rose

Blinded by my own pain I saw only faults
Emptiness and holes stretching like gulfs
Too early I've seen errors of mine too late to erase
Thought I was the hunted but t'was I that led chase
Fueled by a temper sweeping through weakening the storms
I saw only the blood dripping from my rose, onto its thorns
I didn't notice the withering petals until they fell to the ground
I didn't notice all the changes in the rose I carelessly found

Now I go to water it and worse off it's been since

So with it I've been childishly trying to dispense

Out of sane mind, blinded into sight am I

Is there hope to believe my rose won't die?

Overwhelmed

Pain so sickly tangible it seeps through every pore

It trembles every emotion, it shudders to the core

I am not supposed to feel it, separate myself from danger

Separate I from me stop wearing the black dress on the hanger

In solitude I create a river, an abyss

All that's lost can't be spoken can't list

Choking on my own words, like blood was filling my lungs

Like words written to no tune, a song beats with no drums

Incomplete, insufficient to the worlds am I

Completely dried up nothing left inside to cry

Nothing in the world to give leaves nothing you can take

Nothing inside to mold, nothing inside you can break

Still from my pores drip an emotion too strong to cope

Like the calling of the stem to a hopeless fool on dope

Try to break away just for the urge to hit you harder

Tossing you off the path so each day is a day farther

Hold me till the shaking will cease till it passes like the storm

When will it return, the hunger, when will it again swarm

Days of Our Lives

Forever watching, waiting for comprehension to dawn

Waiting for the days of rest, just a glimpse of a yawn

The day comes to a close, the night combined with the sun

When I think I've accomplished just when I think I am done

Another test my way is thrown and bigger must I get

Enemies upon the throne, on top of me I must let

Inside my intestines twist…wrenching my spirit free

Outside the pain is mine, you are you and I am me

Upon our crushed dreams I hope, on this solid ground I slip

No rest, my mind's constant vacation, my soul's eternal trip

Sweet Embraces

When I gaze out these bars I see the sighted leading the sighted

I see the oppression of the soul, of all wisdom, all knowledge

I know not how to smile upon the sickly tangible

I sing not the notes for my voice box is unmanageable

Do I pray to Thee, do I reach, or just let fall

Just opening my heart, just beckoning to His call

Open on command to the world that lies beneath the dirt

Beneath the hunt, the kill, the slaughtered, the hurt

Walking around many times I stumble on legs that won't last

Won't succumb, won't tumble, won't stay, won't grasp

Oops.

Dutiful Daughter

I try and when I do I fail

I cry and when I heal I wail

I open and when I shut you pry

I walk and when I stay I die

Tiring, taking away what I need for my walk

Words fall on deafened ears, how I talk

I hurt and the world is given a feast

I anger then told patience calms the beast

Who calms the hand that throws daggers through?

Cupid's balance is constantly worn by you

I hope and when faith is lost I pray

I pass and when reborn I stay

I am my best when you take and cheat

My worst won't be seen, sit in my seat

Looking Back

No one told me of the echoes that bounce back in time

Surfacing to the beginning the edges of sanity in the mind

Engulfing fog swarming among my limbs, clutching

No one told me of the breakdown reality scarcely touching

Like fall branches and twigs snapping with Pandoric ease

Like our founding fathers fight against any monopolies

No one told me the degrees, temperature dropping

Sick as an addict the heart will soon be stopping

My steps are light faltering only with your stalling

Only one voice, one mind, one soul all calling

Many words with no meaning play upon the Sight's prism

Reacting the chain causing bolts of raging fission

No one told me of the strength I would have to enhance

Speak now or forever hold your piece, alright, last chance

Road Trip

My breath hesitated rocking the center of all I am

I have travelled weary roads, done all that I can

Ruling all that I touch, hearing all that is unsaid, unspoken

Who would've guessed the leader of the pack is easily broken

Taken to one knee as the burden finally took hold

One more scar to add to the soul I have already sold

Purchased by the poor, given with no regret

Hoping for no tomorrow yesterdays hard to forget

Too in tune with internal destruction, like glass I'll break

Confused emotions run past my thoughts, sanity it takes

Paint me a pretty picture of a hurricane and its victims

Place me inside a museum and then display me, prison

Hold the key to my living just outside my grasp

Burn that candle brightly for tonight is my last

I will need to know the way back, the way to home

Again I climb the mountain to inscribe upon stone

My Fable

Light my way; for I am blinded by the darkness

Pull back on those reins hard or me you'll not harness

Catch the tear that holds the wrongs of the whole

Pump the heart, salve the burn and buy the soul

Ink of black, wash away my doubt and my grief

Lock the golden chest, steal the carpet underneath

In my eyes you see no colors, no life behind the glass

No pain beneath the scars, no memories of the past

That haunts this cemetery of the salvation you didn't seek

Recite me lengthy verses of written words you can't speak

The depth you cannot swim because your blood cells explode

Inspiration that uplifts to you never was told

Never was reached out to, no hand in which to grasp

No good book has no end, nothing it seems lasts

Advancing

Would I stop my path if fate did not play?

Would I speak words if to me He didn't say?

Would I shun Love if embracing it wasn't written?

Would I be more personal if for you I wasn't smitten?

If certain liberties of Choice were given as they were to others

Would I want you as my sisters, would I want you as brothers?

If going deaf was an option would I ever hear?

If pain was a courtesy would I still shed a tear?

Choosing going blind or staying sighted

Would I still see, would I still fight it

As children to turn back was fine, was expected

Knowledge was un-owned, wisdom was neglected

As an adult would I commit lessons early on?

Would I not choose to sing this beautiful song?

I have not yet, oh, the test I have in store

Praying for strength can help can reopen the door

Owning courage I'll need before I walk that path

Then I will be granted the justice of his wrath

Acceptance

Through these aged transparent eyes I gaze upon all

With crippled legs I wobble high above, not tall

I surf when I run and jog when I swim

I play the loser yet bred, born to win

Embracing myself with a grasp not too tight

General of the Army, Will not there to fight

Seclusion looking to be a road I won't handle

Conclusions always slipping holder with no candle

Match refusing to spark, striking seems too much

Not holding on, any more you fear the touch

Will it leave, will it end, do not get accustomed

Stick with what I know, terrified to trust Him

Open your path to his lead then you can learn to follow

Fulfillment of your world will come, no longer hollow

No longer settling for that which was never my worth

Never capable of deserving society's definition of hurt

Judge Not Me.

Purpose

Don't try and slice me, I've already bled dry

Don't try to hurt me, the water has been cried

I've already lived within the heat most can't survive

I've clawed my way out, already been buried alive

Went numb so I could feel, died to live

I fear not opening my heart, and give

I defend not from my tests, my trials and my strength

One day you'll go blind to see I'm the type to go the length

I'm the net for your fall, the ladder for your climb

I fit the needs you serve at this point in your time

Not afraid to speak for justice, to fight for right

Wanting to befriend those that can't help but fight

Apologies not given for failures not committed

Not a child to convince my Will no longer submitted

Be by my side, walk with me the rest of the road

Write it upon your soul this can be our story told

I cannot wear the dress on the hanger to me you hand

I will not take two steps back from the view I now stand

Either way I lose as Life has taught me is its humor

Winning not a word, competition is just a rumor

Take my exposed palm but don't accept my purity of heart

Wish I could reminisce but no longer can you tear me apart

Judge harshly on a world where your control no longer reigns

Shun my sincerity when no longer you can inflict any pain

Though I wish another way, reality must have different plans

Tell me I am welcome then hand me a long list of all my bans

Then watch me fall down to knees weathered with lost souls

You are my very breath, without you, I have no goals

Ridiculousness

When daylight slams into the darkness of the night

When wings of the eagle break, no longer is flight

No longer is freedom when the cell is within

Salvation a mirage when the religion is sin

Practiced by all they love to worship, to praise

Love confusion, love being lost, in a daze

Then gaze upon me as if strange finally was defined

Slaughter me with words conveyed to you with my mind

Every thought dripping down, until the soul is drenched

Until anger is what remains after reason away I wrenched

Ask me for it back, persist until I bend

The rest will do the same sheep and their trends

To have all the keys but still you knock and scream

Still you wonder on the answers, still you dream

Sense out of chaos, hah, you forgot to carry the one

When the moon's beam bleeds into blazing rays of sun

Define Awesome.

The dawn is coming closer, the dark undisturbed

Feelings overwhelming and the wrath remains uncurbed

Fear courses slowly, the lazy meandering pace making me nauseous

The hope suffocating the wisdom, overriding my nature of cautious

Stepping upon my head, tromping my already beaten vessels

My already insane mind wrestles no more with mundane riddles

Pain no longer felt in a fortress fortified with unrelenting flames

The blaze that is a whisper from the cold lips for most it claims

Then come upon the stares of the stupefied that claim comprehension

Igniting, my insecurities slapping like a restless sheet in the wind

Nowhere to turn but down, to the bottom, on my knees

Humility rocking my soul, majority of self did not please

Save Me

Happiness and comfort, luxuries for those not seeing

For those not willing, for those outside the being

Open me up to shut all the doors

Dress me up like one of your whores

Treat me with respect you reflect in your mirror

Shove me from your ambience, grab me pull me nearer

I will grasp the air, thinning before my empty sockets

Only sipping air from the drowned' air pockets

Taking a breath from stale air, taking a step towards broken bridges

All the while I say I am inhaling, inside I know my breath hitches

Pollution of the soul too great to unwind

Too much in plain sight for the commoner to find

Pen drown the sound, the screams, the echoes of lost words

The shout from the spirit my deafened ears have heard

I will come.

Stay Hungry

I stay blinded so I can be among the seeing

I stay faithless so I can be among the believing

I stay trapped in this concrete so freedom will be mine

I stay within this rhyme

I hold onto the anguish surrounding my past

I hold onto the temporary for the memories that last

I hold onto no one so loneliness is my friend

I hold on until the end

I fight these emotions that cannot be released

I fight back the urge to puke from the stench of disease

I fight the injustices that pollute my lungs, my breath

I fight until the death

I stand among those that kneel on blistered knees

I stand for stupidity to find wisdom that never leaves

I stand for questions so answers will arrive with proof

I stand for the truth

Tomorrow Comes

The pain of losing you

Every day I walk and go through the motions

Every day I talk and hide my deeper emotions

Every day I wonder if today is the day

When floods cease and clouds go away

If the sun will shine upon this soul, so numb

If peace will clear this mind, rest will come

Carry me once more for to my knees I've fallen again

I beg for shelter promised that will keep out the wind

Every day that closes survival I have achieved
Every day I wonder where I'd be without belief
If this hasn't made me stronger then here I would not remain
If all the work was done then the Angels too would call my name
If more beauty to offer the world, I had not
My precious spirit St. Peter by now would have sought
Trust in Him is what you fortify, though painful is the how
Strength is what you teach, then, during, now
The joy of losing you

Truth Indefinitely

Have I matured, have I weathered this pen?
Did the ink take me like the insanities of men?
Did the wisdom held at such a tender age fade?
Did the fight leave me during my path, my crusade?
You ask questions once again, time must've stood still
Always waiting on answers, never understanding your will
Never exercising anything past the suffering and pain
Knowledge not applied, is knowledge not gained
Look past my wall of words deep into our soul
Then ask again, did time take a toll?
Not possible.

Timely Reminders

Choosing to be foe instead of friend
Wanting only beginnings never ends
Helps me to find my pulse, my emotion

Helps me sort through thoughts, my notions

Elevating the rate of my heart you make me once again feel

Complacent I became in life, forgetting the sense of real

The sense of touched as in deep to the core

No longer existing in the pain, the sore

Now understanding the tingle sliding over my skin

Does not only have to come from tears or from sin

Alive I become as joy and knowledge replace the dark

Clothed I feel as deeply where before it took stark

Bare to the universe I will remain but always guarded

Stern to my brothers is survival not hardened

Whole I can be and remain in tune with sky and earth

Truth is found when death circles back around to birth

Clocking In

Do you understand what I mean by the call of the pen?

The demand on my soul it takes now, and then

The revelations that are revealed can be unclear

The voice that is spoken, do you really hear?

Deafened am I by the confusion that is elected

Blinded am I by the light that is rejected

Humbled am I by the soul that is not yet saved

The words of this pen that continually have me enslaved

The ink that slowly drips into the subconscious frame of mind

Words that grasp my throat from another place, another time

The quill that drenches my person, my entirety, my vessel

No cookie cutter rhymes, no tracing, no stencils

With this pen I have no equal alone I will always remain

It allows me to put it down so I can come in from all the rain

The same that soaked me then is not as heavy, not as torrential

Claims not the same space, the same mass, providential

It's just wet.

Sweet

And so I breathe in when breathing slices

And so I mush on when no one else fights it

When no one else reaches the depths, too deep

Too dark is the hole where dehydrated we weep

Where upon the stone where laws are writ

Where upon my palm Truth was spit

Upon my head the moon and stars

Twinkling to the tune strung out of my heart

Carved into a surface time can seek but not burn

Underneath the world that long ago ceased to turn

Living smited like the innocence once found in a babe

Became man, the boundaries, the appetite, wayward slave

Come home to me, will you not ask, not see

Do not see, do not ask, come home to me

Choppy Waters

The future is looming and my breath shortens

My mind spinning in an unstoppable vortex

My hearts drums so loud and sweat drips to its beat

Sliding down my body, pooling at my feet

Leaving my eyes dry only my soul is able to weep

Only resting children hear the sobs in their sleep

Waited centuries to spew this word unto the worlds

Holding breath after breath until my lungs shrivel and curl

Until the heat from the blaze gave me life once again

To transfer what you can't grasp from this mind to this pen

Where are those that need to read because starved is their life

Alone is their company, honesty their strife

I will beckon at the time where no time exists

I will strike with the fury of an armless man's fists

I will tell you stories of old to help bring in the new

Let me be your beacon, let me help you through

Soon

Shall I tell you the whispers that float through my brain?

Shall I impart the death and rape that is to come again?

Men that claw at their face just to reach their eyes

Men that rip out their throat just to reach their cries

The wicked that will reign and the sheep that will follow

The emptying of emotions so that the spirit is hollow

The eagerness you will show that will break my heart in two

The endless prayers and sins that I must commit for you

How much have I spared you but even I cannot

Stop that that doesn't exist by stopping the hands on the clock

Upon the skies of the tombs of all that live

Here is my confession what more shall I give

Shall I tell you of the secrets that are ancient and pure?

Shall I hand to you the bottle that contains the cure?

Men that poison their minds with definitions falsely taught

Men that run to prison when their self is already caught

Already abandoned for greener pastures where grass is dried and dead

Men that cut off their hands just to reach their head

When it is written to come for you I will sacrifice my heart

Could you swallow death and find the healing of the dark?

Should've, Would've, Could've

Should I tell you of what I can't see, don't know?

Should I give to you what is not mine, can't show?

Should I open to you what is never closed, no key?

Should I show you a mirror with no reflection, not me?

I would

Should I hold you with stone arms gently now?

Should I feel you without touch, show you how?

Should I light for you a candle, no home?

Should I bow to you and serve, cold throne?

I could

Mount Up

Do you see the tremble beneath the skin?

The plates shifting and settling within

What of the fireflies that drop in the air

The spots of light falling here and there

You cannot see because your vision remains

You cannot feel until numbness is gained

You cannot hurt when pain is a state of mind

A state of heart, of spirit, of time

So the flames that constantly licks at my feet

Cannot possible burn or make me weep

So the fire that once drove me mad and deep

Rip out my vocal cords so unto you I can speak

Do you see the enlightenment that I paid for dearly?

Loss of beliefs, of faith, of life very nearly

Is my soul aged enough can you see into my eyes

Look upon me with hollow sockets conquer your despise

Command your emotions so we can have one hope

One voice, one mind, one way to bind this rope

That slithers up my carcass and heads to end my breath

Like yesterday; today; tomorrow, one death

Loss of Innocence

To me once you were a poem

Wondrous creek water flowing

My secret hopes I placed before you

My dreams sparkled in your sea of blue

Then the storm came crashing in

Slicing deep through weathered skin

Thrashing my beings to and fro

Reality dawning, definition of foe

Feeble mindedly I grasp onto definitions of old

Boiling over in the pot, hot water to scold

Reminder of burns from memory past

Changes upon my character here to last

All that I gave to a soul choosing to be damned

All that I am, tested, torn, unmanned

Seemingly clear now, redefining behind walls

More cuts and scrapes then a child's fall

If knowledge is power, then costly is power

Weight won't bend me these shoulders don't cower

Wolves in sheep's clothing

Back to One

The whistle blows again so I am to be taken

Through emotions that once before were forsaken

Through the motions of living, to the brink

Sliming its way through arteries this dark ink

Grab tightly onto this pen that will call to the worlds

That will call for the justice, all lies to be unfurled

Will you beckon or will you run?

Will you leave or will you come?

The outer shell will fall away, regret will be evoked

Time for flamed sacrifice is done now only ash and smoke

Protectors unite; warriors unsheathe your sharp menacing blades

Soulless vessels depart; clock striking twelve on the unsaved

 Harmonizing, the sound of the end will be one song

The sins of man combined, see only one wrong

With my one voice I will pray; with this one tear I will weep

Tragedies and secrets contained in this one mind I'll keep

Damnation and enlightenment become the same viral infection

Affecting the beat of this one heart, slowing palpitations

Peaceful dreams wreak nightmarishly havoc in the subconscious, deep

Take this pillow, take this blanket and settle yourself down to our one sleep

Dazed and Confused

My mind is circling around a concept it cannot grasp

My head is pounding from the spinning that is so fast

My heart is racing like a meth-induced frenzy

My soul is pouring out like a man on bended knee

My laugh is hollow like the chambers within this heart

My cry is smothered inside me nothing sparks

A tomb couldn't be this cold, this deep this dry

A wound could not be any more open than I

A friend cannot come from rubble and trash

A hand cannot help my stumble, my crash

A hope cannot be when light finds no way

Dazed and confused I will wander astray

I Can Live

You are so deep inside me that your joy is my pain

You are so connected to me, my blood and your veins

I am so deep inside you that my strengths are your fears

I am so connected to you, your pain and my tears

Life will always give us obstacles; test our boundaries and our bond

Truth is the only thing that keeps what we have together going strong

Many claim to give their lives to the ones that they love the best

What I give to you is life, confirmed by the results of the HIV test

I stand before you not guessing, knowledge is the best gift I can give

Know that the life we build will be greater if I know for me you live

Many vows we will make

Few promises will we break

Show me you can live for me too

The Rift That Ties

The land speaks through the wind, the wind to soul

The trees dancing to the story that is being told

Centuries have come together in land torn apart

Green as deep as envy, soil as red as the heart

Pumping inspiration into veins gathered at artistic rubble

Stealing words, stealing breath, replacing both with humble

Random Thought ** (written as a song)

When I met you, you were somebody else

When I held you, you were holding yourself

When I told you that I loved, you just played along

Now you're gone and all I have left is this song

C: I can't be anybody but myself

          I can't wish from the bottom of your well

          I have no quarters to spare

          No change left to give

          Just myself, that's all I have left

Past Love (written as a song)

Love makes the world go round

But lately things have slowed down

We don't caress each other's bodies

And we don't ease each other's minds

I don't want just anybody

But with you love is hard to find

C: Oh love is a good thing

          If you keep it living

Yes we have to find our groove thing

We have to start giving

But love can be a bad thing

If only you wants it to last

So we have to start living and we have to start giving or our love it will be in the past

You're fronting and you don't seem to realize

When you talk I got passion in my eyes

Why do you do what you do when your boys are hanging round

The way you show your love baby it's turning me upside down

C:

You think we can just stop talking and we can just kick on back

But boy you're gonna start walking when our love becomes a think of the past

C:

Love Is (written as a song)

Loving you humbles me

Loving you till I can breath

Loving you eternally

Loving you till I can see

Everything I do

Everything I say

Every single night

Every single day

Has a whisper of you baby

I just can't seem to get you outta my head

Your scent, your touch every single word that you said

It haunts my soul

It steals my breath

Every day before knowing you I was living in death

You're my breath of fresh air

You're my beach on a moonlit night

I'm the wind that plays in your hair

I'm the feeling in your heart when everything's alright

All I need is you

All you need is me

Baby take my hand

Walk this road and see

The rest of our lives baby

Loving you humbles me

Loving you till I can't breath

Loving you eternally

Loving you till I can't see

Random Thought ** (written as a song)

I played around with destiny

I tempted the God's of fate

And they brought me to my knees

Now I'm begging help me please

Heal my heart

My soul, my entirety

I'm not trying to justify myself

Or what I've done

I don't want pity from the world, the father, the son

I just want you to know

That I'm sorry

Please forgive me

Just leave me to walk in the darkness of loneliness

Move on